At the Races

Acknowledgments

Thanks to the editors of the following, in which some of these poems first appeared:

London Magazine, *The North*, *Other Poetry*, *Poetry Ireland Review*, *The Rialto*, *The SHOp*, *Stride*, and *The Tablet*. 'The Fields' won the Leslie Richardson Award.

Some of these poems appeared in the pamphlet *Cold Hill Pond* (Smith/Doorstop Books, 2007).

Also by Michael McCarthy:

Birds' Nests and Other Poems (Bradshaw books)
The Story Of Noah and the Ark (Barefoot Books)
The Story of Daniel and the Lion's Den (Barefoot Books)

For Shirley

With best Wishes

At the Races
Michael McCarthy

Michael McCarthy

Smith/Doorstop Books

Published 2009 by
Smith/Doorstop Books
The Poetry Business
Bank Street Arts
32-40 Bank Street
Sheffield S1 2DS
www.poetrybusiness.co.uk

ISBN 978-1-906613-09-9

British Library Cataloguing-in-Publication Data.
A catalogue record for this book is available from the
British Library.

Typeset by Utter
Printed in Great Britain by the MPG Books Group,
Bodmin and King's Lynn
Cover design by Utter
Author photograph © Michelle Neville

Smith/Doorstop Books is a member of Inpress,
www.inpressbooks.co.uk. Distributed by Central Books
Ltd., 99 Wallis Road, London E9 5LN.

The Poetry Business gratefully acknowledges the help of
Arts Council England.

Supported by
ARTS COUNCIL
ENGLAND

At the Races won the 2008/9 Poetry Business
Competition judged by Michael Longley.

For the people among whom I grew up,

and for you who have sustained me

in life and in poetry.

CONTENTS

THE FIELDS

Before Aunt Nora ever sent me that prayer book
with the red cover, before *St Albert the Great*
and *The Man Who Got Even With God*, before
school books and books from the Library Van
I was reading the fields and the run of the land.

The pathway that ran straight as a story
through the middle of the field below the house
coming to a full stop at the well. The pond
where the gander ruled and the geese hissed
the hill-field, and the meadow with the chained bull.

The brake, its folds dressed forever in yellow furze
with spiders hiding in their nylon webs. Pairc na Phurt,
the bog, the field where the rabbits sat on the rock
and the Camlach field, and the road that ran down
to the inches, to the river singing its own song.

The big inch where we learned to swim, the coarse inch
where we galloped the horse, the long inch where
the hares had their set and the flood came out,
and the spot where my father hid, up to his nose
after drowning the dog, the time of the Black and Tans.

The gravel field with the dug-out where they slept,
the briar field, Catherine's bog, Conaic na Muc,
Graif na Linnga, Claishe Ghapail, the fields by the road,
the field at the cross. The Moonaideen, Pairc na Bharrica,
the cabbage garden, and the field in front of the house.

Fields where cows grazed in summer then trudged home
weighed down with milk; where heifers stood stock-still
under trees, drizzle gathering like jewels on their backs.
The field where the fox jumped out through the ferns
brazen as the sky with a hen in his mouth.

Fields in spring where potato drills were lines on a page.
Autumn fields lyrical with oats, verses of barley in stooks .
Turnips in winter fields, exclamation marks on frozen ground.
They're all one field now, ditches a thing of the past.
Under my bare feet still the grammar of the grass.

OUR HOUSE

In the hallway: a holy water font on the door jamb.
On the hall-stand your father's hat. Beside the stairs
– linoleum covered with brass rods – a picture (a woman
in a blue dress) with verse: The Road of Friendship,
and framed, a list of names: West Cork's Heroic Dead.

In the kitchen: the fireplace between twin hobs.
On the range – Modern Mistress – a kettle and large pot.
From the chimney the smell of soot. On the clevy:
a come-lately radio, a tea caddy with sailors, sugar
in a Fox's Mint jar. Nine rosary beads hang from a hook.

On the wall: the clock with key inside. A lamp flickering
before the Sacred Heart. Next to the settle bed, a bucket
with spring water. A dark ring on the ceiling over the Tilley lamp.
On the dresser: a jug of milk, large Wilton patterned plates,
glue marks where a tinker repaired the cracks.

In the parlour: a big round table, six horsehair chairs, one broken.
A chaise longue. Chiffonier with purple breakfast cups and china set.
Silver teapot. Another, elephant-shaped, with black woman riding on top.
A clock on the mantel-piece, the time always at five o clock.
On the wall: your parents wedding; a picture of your brother aged ten.

BELOW THE WELL

Mushrooms grow wild in the round field,
The dewy grass hides each bald head.

You can pick a few and bring them home,
As many in your hands as there is room.

Don't put them in your pocket, you'll forget
and they'll only get bruised and break.

Peel them, lay them on the range, let them sit.
Watch their pink ridges darken and go flat.

When they start to sizzle put them on a plate,
Let them cool, then sprinkle them with salt.

Lift them up with a fork, don't spill the juice.
Shape your lips like you were giving a kiss.

They'll be like the host on your tongue only hot
and they won't stick to the roof of your mouth.

TO SCHOOL

Summer time and the short sleeves, and no shoes
and rabbits bobbing west-side of Sean Neill's bog.
Dew on the grass, and the gap in the ditch,
and frog spawn in the long-go flax pond,
and the water-works and the briars by the big tank
and smoke from Johnny Noonan's one chimney.
The faucet like a small fountain beside the river
where Mrs Noonan gets the water for their tea,
where we drum our feet on the wooden bridge

and race up Kingston's field past the stall and the shed,
the house and cherry tree, and down to Carraig a Thonnaig.
'Your father slept there during the troubles,' Willie says.
Then up the hill past the hazel tree and the high ditch
to the rutted road, and away below us the river's rush.

Across the valley Harnedy's house hides in the trees.
We catch up to Den Brien on his way to the creamery
with his slow horse and iron wheel cart and churns
that clang as he goes along, and Den deaf as a stone.
He tells us to sit in. The big iron wheels turn slowly,
the churns lurch at every turn, we fear for our fingers
and toes. It takes forever to get up Paul Sam Jim's hill.
At Dempsey's gravel pit we know we'll be dead late,
like being after the Gospel getting into Mass.

At Miah Charley's cross Den pulls in, lets
Jim Carthy swish past in his rubber wheeled cart.
At Chrioshe na Marb there's no sound because
they've all gone in to school. He lets us off
at the humped back bridge. We say thanks for the lift.
The master will surely give us a slap.

12

BLUE JUMPER

My mother knit it during the summer
specially for going to school.
She measured it against me at bed time
making sure it would fit like a shell.
It was blue as the August sky
and had double ridges down the front
that weaved in and out like fish-tails.

When I tried it on the sleeves hugged me
and the v neck was heaven. It was fit
for the High King of Ireland, or a hero
like Padraig Pearse. I felt like a hero myself.

But the teacher didn't notice,
never asked who knit it,
or gave me a sweet.

In the evening we lined up for singing:
God save Ireland said the heroes.
She didn't even notice me then.
I stood by the wall in the sunlight
stroking the ridges. It was almost
like stroking the cat's back.
She got the ruler out of her drawer
came over and gave me a slap.

The stinging in my hand tingled
like the sound of the tuning fork,
or the swimming of a far off bell.
Then they began to sing: *Glory-o*
Glory-o, to the bold Fenian Men.

LEARNING

You remember nothing about grammar. Or maths, except
seven times tables: *Seacht fe seacht sin dahad a naoi*,
and nothing at all about Irish apart from that.
Or English. Or poetry except for Padraig Pearse:
Mother Ireland I have loved thee
with a love that knew no fear.

Bits of history: 1014, Brian Boru beating the Danes
at the battle of Clontarf. Domnal O' Sullivan's march
to O' Rourke of Breiffne, after breaking the siege at Dunboy.
The Annals of the Four Masters had the sound of a book you'd like.

Religion: Catechism class, the Master talking about
immodest dress, you wondering what class of a dress was that?
Parables, 'put them into your own words'
– there was a farmer one time had two sons.

Compositions, but not what they were about, or what you wrote.
Ink wells, ha-penny nibs, Teresa Dennigan licking the ink off hers
for fear she'd make a blot. Her mouth all blue like she was
after eating blackberries, and her big brother Peadar
pouring a full inkwell down his throat, like men
throwing back a glass of whiskey at a wake.

What you remember best: the slopes of the school yard
and the high hedge; and the wall dividing the boys from the girls
with a hole near the gable; and eating your lunch: the bottle of milk
and the taste of brown bread and blackberry jam; and the Regans
having theirs out of a box; and O' Brien's mother bringing him
a boiled egg in a stocking to keep it hot.

Brigadier 'The O' Donovan' arriving with a pile of *National Geographic*,
and saying 'jolly good' this and 'jolly good' that, and the Master
getting the class to stand up and sing. *The Boys of Kilmichael*
a song the Brigadier said he'd never heard.

The bikes and riders in the *Ras Tailtean* whizzing past.
One rider clinging onto someone else's handlebars, another
miles after everyone else. 'A puncture' Mickey Dineen said,
'either that or his chain came off. He'll never again catch up.'

HEADING HOME

Most days we run helter skelter up the old road, wooden pencil-cases
rattling in our school bags like dancers on Ceidhli hour. Today though
the Bawnahow crowd have called us cowards. Hiding behind a furze bush
I watch my brother stand his ground, give them a dressing they won't forget.

We hurry on east. Miah Charley is having an argument with his horse.
D.J.Dempsey is making concrete blocks. We take Mrs Dempsey *The Far East*.
We get a cut of currant cake. Paulie has mashed potatoes with yellow sweets
around the edge of the plate, and two red squirrels in a glass case.

We pick hazel nuts, crack them open with a stone, eat the white flesh.
Carraig a Thonnaig is wild and steep, how did the men on the run get any sleep
Mrs Kingston gives us bastible bread with sugar sprinkled on top.
She says, 'run away home now or ye'll be late.'

At the foot-bridge we stop half way across. Leaning over the wooden parapet
we stare down at the water. When the bridge starts to move we hold on tight.
We sail away to China and Japan. When it goes too fast we shut our eyes
to make it stop, then run like mad, each of us trying to be home first.

KNITTING

There was always knitting going on in our house.
My sisters started young.
My mother never stopped.
I helped roll the spools of wool into a ball
with my hands stretched out
like the priest when he was saying Mass.

Kitty Kelly came visiting my sisters.
She joined in. She stuck the ball of wool
inside her cardigan. They all giggled.
I said our teacher, Mrs Fitzgerald
had two apples under her jumper.
Her jumper was knitted in a shop.

They were all laughing when I said that.
They told me to go and play outside.
My mother didn't laugh when I told her
about Kitty Kelly and the ball of wool.
When I told her about Mrs Fitzgerald
and the apples she gave a smile.

Later on it got all mixed up.
Adam and Eve. The serpent. Apples.
The delicate indecencies of the moon.

JANUARY

This time of year is not the time for making jam.
The blackberries are long gone, the briars withered
and lying there, worn out and stringy in the hollows.
No longer leaning across a gap to catch you as you run
into the next field leaving you with your legs laddered,
the ground all sodden with cow trod and horse gallop.

Shoeing horses is a January job, and snaring rabbits,
and having stir-about for supper. All that damp
and squelch and suck of wellingtons in mud changes
come the frost, to the ring of hobnailed boots across
the yard, and frost nails gripping on the cobbles.
And plovers down from the hills, dressed like Sunday,
proud as women on their way to Mass. And at night
sheets of frozen mirrors wink back at the stars.

'CLIMBING MOUNT EVEREST' BY SIR EDMUND HILLARY

My father didn't like the Sir, it was like God Save the Queen.
And he thought climbing mountains was no trial of a man.
'There isn't much *meas* on that class of thing around here.'

I carried on reading all the same, tagging along
Behind Hillary and Tensing. Oxygen masks,
Tackle, ropes, all the gear, crampons,
Even though I didn't know what they were.

Sunday evening, somewhere between the apple tree
And the gooseberry bush, we set out from base camp.
At twenty nine thousand feet and snow-blind
I could feel the freezing inside of my skin.
I was climbing higher and higher into the thin air
When my father shouted: "Michael. Go for the cows."

Milking the cow in the southern stall
I imagined our final assault. The spurts of milk
On the base of the metal bucket was the sough of the wind.
The sounds growing hollow and hoarse as the bucket filled
Were our footsteps crunching the snow, our rasping for breath.

Resting below the summit, the milk almost up to the rim
The cow rolled in a great avalanche pinning me to the wall.
The bucket went flying. The milk spread like a sudden thaw,
The snow of my mountain-top melting into the straw.

Years later I read, the first thing Hillary said was:
"We knocked the bastard off." I liked that.

What I like now: how Tensing knelt on the snow
On the summit of Chomolungma, the home of the gods.

SMOKING

I've never smoked, except that one time
when I found a fag in a Gold Flake box
my father thought was finished. I left it until
Sunday night when the rest of them were gone
to the dance. I listened to the top twenty first
then snuck it inside my shirt and headed off
down the boreen to the bottom of the hill.

There beside the well where the horses drank
I lit up and gave a pull. I watched it redden,
then giddily blew the smoke out of my mouth.
Number one was *Stranger on the Shore*
by Mr Acker Bilk. The excitement was
knowing I wouldn't be found out. Next thing
a yellow hammer flew out of a furze bush.

I'm glad now that I never took it up
but I'd like to see another yellow hammer
and I wouldn't mind listening to Mr Acker Bilk.

THAT SUMMER

I can't remember if it was the year of the Congo
when Patrice Lumumba was assassinated in Katanga.
Or the year of Shan Mohangi who murdered his girlfriend
Hazel Mullen: her body found under The Green Tureen in Dublin.

What I do remember: the rows of desks, and my green trousers smooth
against the shine of the seat, and Cronin over by the window brushing
his crew-cut. And the after-taste of salty porridge the nun with the hood
and the smiling breast plate had handed through the hatch that morning.

I remember remembering what my father said to the postman:
'You'll have war' and the postman adding 'and rationing?'
But I can not remember how exactly, that fight started.
Davy Barry and I were the best of friends.

How it was that the jostling turned serious as we pushed back and forth
not noticing the circle form and the crowd climbing onto the desks
until the shout 'scrap on' grew into a din and we were caught,
neither of us having the bottle to bottle out?

I remember the knot in my stomach; his face drained, fear in his eyes,
and someone shouting 'come on Davy'. I don't remember who landed
first, only the frenzy of flying fists, the sting of my cut knuckle, and
the sudden amazement of blood pumping out of his mouth.

'Nix,' someone hissed, just before the priest appeared on the steps.
Next day when I saw him with cut lips and shoulders slumped
he wouldn't look me in the eye, or speak. I felt very sorry
for the loser, very glad it wasn't myself.

ENGLISH EXAM

I was a bowl of odds before the start.
They all said John Masefield was a cert.
I'd learned everything about Sea Fever by heart

It was Cargoes came up. I knew Cargoes
Began with Quinquirème, which I couldn't spell,
And had amethysts, Isthmus, and Topazes,
which I couldn't pronounce, never mind spell.

'Write an appreciation of Cargoes
Quoting the poem in full.'
I said I certainly appreciated Cargoes, but
I thought Sea Fever was oceans ahead.

I said Sea Fever was a class of a disease.
I MUST go down to the seas again, to the lonely sea and the sky,
Anyone who read the poem would catch the disease.
And anyone who'd never even seen the sea could see why.

I must go down to the seas again, for the call of the running tide
I said Masefield had it so bad he was in a lather of sweat,
Is a wild call and a clear call that may not be denied;
Like that time I got the measles, only different.

Sea Fever was contagious, without
a cure I said, and I was willing to bet
John Masefield wasn't in the better of it yet.

*

When I read the next question I knew I'd lost the score.
'A historical figure, supporting your essay with facts'.
I couldn't think of any figure, and I wasn't good on facts.
So I made one up. I made up the facts as well.

I re-invented my father. I wrote everything I knew about him
And a lot that I didn't. That he was a hero of the Flying Column.
That his name was Timsy Mc Andrew and he was a fright.
That he shot forty Black and Tans in one night.

Afterwards they were all saying they'd written about Parnell,
Michael Collins, or Padraig Pearse. One fella wrote about Churchill.
When Fr Kiely asked who I'd written about I admitted what I'd done.
'Good man yourself,' was all he said. I was a bowl of odds again.

THE MORNING BOBBY KENNEDY DIED

The Dalmatics, red, gold, purple, off white
have been allocated in pairs. Steve and I
get the green ones. Eamonn and Billy
are in red. Dr Seeldrayers is giving the organ
full throttle as we process in. The ceremony
lasts two hours, and when we come back out
it's done. We're in it now for the long haul.
Next year will be Ordination proper.

Mc Mahon with the rust coloured hair
is at the door offering congratulations.
'Allow me Mick'. 'You're allowed.'
A few of the boys have lit up with relief.
I'm smiling in the afterglow of it.
The organ has followed us outside
mixing in with the smell of laburnum
and cut grass. The sky is overcast.
Someone says Bobby Kennedy is dead.
I didn't even know he'd been shot.

SHROGGS PARK HALIFAX 1970

The park is quiet today. The steps
on the miniature basilica are damp,
its roof wrapped in a green scarf of moss.
The fountain, switched off for months, has mould
on the metal. There's a smell of dead leaves.

A woman walks her dog, a poodle
dressed up in a jacket and clipped to the ears,
white, with dirty feet. The woman wears a brown hat.
We pretend we're not watching each other:
me, still new, in my black suit and anorak.

Beyond the fringe of rhododendrons
the outcrop of rock gives way suddenly.
A steep gravel-path winds down through
the puzzle of tree trunks and bare branches
to the road where car roofs come and pass.

Across in the valley, the refuse dump.
A digger moves under a canopy of seagulls,
back and forth, treating it all the same.
A bin-liner full of old shoes, an enamel jug.
I think of elsewhere. Ploughed fields, horses.

SHILLELAGH

'Keep it beside your bed' she says, showing me
the shine on it. 'That's what I've done with it
all my life. After setting the table for breakfast,
after feeding the cat, after getting the rent money
out of his brother on a Thursday night. Coppers
I called his brother. *Hey up, where's me coppers.*

You wouldn't know what they'd be up to
around here son. Put that beside your bed
and God help any burglar tries to break in.
That there cracked Protestant skulls in 1912.
My mother gave it to me for my wedding.
I haven't had to use it much.'

37 GRASMERE DRIVE

Discarded items lie half hidden in the garden.
A tricycle. An upturned pram, its wheels missing.
A black dog is curled up on the thrown-out couch.
The boy is about eight, his face round as the sun.

'Is your mother in?' I ask.
'Are you the man from the YEB?'

His mother hasn't paid her bill, and for a good reason.
They've cut her off. Mr O' Hara who lives next door
has kindly connected her to the meter in his house,
which is connected to the one in the next house.

'I'm not from the YEB,' I tell him. 'I'm the priest.'
'Hold on, I'll find out if she's in.'

'We're not Catholics' he says when he comes back.
'You're down here as Catholics,' I say, waving my book.
'We used to be but now we're not. Mum says she's not in.'
'That's fine,' I say. 'Tell her I'm not here.'

OLIVE

Often, the sheets are storm tossed.
Angled elbows, knees, protrude at random. Sometimes
A turbulence of limbs breaks through the surface.
Once, her chest exposed, a withered nipple
Intimated I should look away.

Her spirit is a ship long sunk. Never a hint
Of recognition. I come here to pray with her.
Searching downward – in the blind chance
A prayer might reach her – I stand helpless.
Olive, you are no advert for old age.

Today, a nurse has been to tidy up
The bedclothes smooth and restful.
A radio plays in the background
Rod Stewart, raucous yet melodic:
Have I told you lately that I love you.

THEOLOGICALLY SPEAKING

i.m Tess Carr 1921–2003

The Church: there beside the lake
hunchbacked against the wind
since eighteen-fifty-four.

In the background
Cardinal Wiseman's cedar
growing taller every year.

Close by: the grass cut
the undergrowth cleared away
the small wooden cross now obvious.

'Who's buried here?' I ask.
'Bernadette', she says.
My eyebrows puzzle.
'The cat.'

Realising this wasn't your average cat
I hesitate. 'It's not a matter
of being small-minded or anything
but theologically speaking
Jesus didn't die for cats.
Could the grave be marked say by a shrub?'

Over a medium-sized pause
my suggestion is dismissed.

'She did enough for this Church.
Everybody loved that cat.'

Theology would have to please itself.
May Bernadette have eternal rest.

SAXTON CHURCHYARD

To Edward, and in memory of Amy

Close to where Lord Dacre was buried
beside his horse after the battle of Towton
your family and friends gather in a half-circle
your Mum & Dad next to the small white box.
In front of them an array of bouquets:

Gingerbread-man with silver sleeves,
a bear in purple jump-suit, a cake
with interlocking hearts, each
accompanied by its love note.

You, still in your ventilator at the LGI
weighing in at just over two pounds
and armed only with your wrist band
are fighting your own battles.

On this day of loss, and clear June light
the tall priest, in white alb and stole
soothes out his words. Above him
in the ancient yew tree, a thrush
singing her heart out.

ROOM AT THE INN

By the time the wise men arrive
the car park is full. Balthazar's Dad
parks in front of Mr Thornhill's drive.
Mr Thornhill says 'Excuse Me.' His face is red.

Melchior's Mum has parked two streets away
having dropped him off at the door.
When she gets back he tells her
he's left his Myrrh in the car.

Inside, parents line the side aisles
digital cameras at arm's length.
Joseph's step-father has a video cam.
He has snakes tattooed on his neck.

Mary smiles from under her blue veil
as she gazes down on the infant child.
Joseph kneels, proud as any father
his painted sideburns Elvis to an L.

The shepherds stand wide-eyed, carrying sticks,
their stuck-on beards glistening in the spotlight.
(One of the sheep has failed to turn up on the night.)
Gabriel sits at the side, checking his mobile for text.

The choir of angels sing a medley of songs
Jingle all the way followed by *Silent Night*.
Afterwards the reindeer brothers have fish and chips.
One of them drinks too much fizz, throws up on the steps.

REMEMBERING HANYANG

My uncle sways under a half hid moon
his ribcage cranked, his papers missing.
Wakening, surprised to find he's home
he rises and walks out in the night.

In China he travelled from the sacred river
to the hills, where the sky opened
and closed at random, and distance blurred
in the continent of his eyes.

In the beginning when neither time nor space
told him anything, there were only the whispering
indifferent currents, and from the horse's thick
brown coat the smell of saddle-sweat.

His mouth clay-clammed, his tongue
a foreign language, light glittering
from his frozen shoes, his black socks
holed and heavy with a sweat gone cold.

He taught them how Moses travelled dry-shod
through the sea, and how in ancient
Ireland, Patrick ran the snakes
forever from the land.

Here, now, a meadow stilled in daylight.
Remembering Hanyang. Kidnappers
desperate for a windfall; horses
who were never fed on furze.

IN THE BEGINNING

In the beginning was the Word
and the Word was the beginning
the not yet spoken spoken
the untold toldness telling

and the Word was a breath
a small spill of breath
tongue-touched into a whisper
from the beginnings of breathing

and the whisper lingered
ebbed itself over the riverbanks
out of the deepest gullies
between the swill of water and water

and the waters mirrored
the Word that was a breath
the breath that was a whisper
that became the Word in the beginning.

and the Word grew bright
in all the galaxies
in the mirror of waters
among the tall grasses
.
A man came, a man John.
He was not the light
but the light was in him
so that his dark breath brightened

and the stab of light
was a pillar in the valley
an arch over the holly
a shine on the wet berry

it hovered over the trees
swung from branch to branch
leaped on the hard ground
until the earth shuddered

and the Word laughed
and the Word wept
and the Word became flesh
as it was in the beginning.

NODDFA

Perched above the shoreline, the house
set among cedars, arbutus, horse chestnut.
In the far corner a fountain,
the water rounded to a perfect globe
of blown glass that catches the sun at random.

Small gusts of wind burst it momentarily
turning the misted spray to rainbow.
Retreatants move at the pace of prayer
their silence broken only by birdsong.

By the door, among shrubbery: wisteria
hollyhocks, fuchsia, a bee in his yellow
striped prison garb forages for nectar.
A honey coloured cat meditates on the doorstep.

*

In the hallway, the tiled floor opens
onto the wide stairwell. Beyond it
a narrow corridor leads to the stone chapel

and there, on a teak table, among
potted plants, and a jar of pink petunias
the statue of the pregnant virgin

her chin raised, her hair tied back,
the mound of child prominent, under
the waterfall of her long green dress.

Around her feet a circle of small shells
their ears to the ground. Any moment
now, the waters break.

TRANSFIGURATION

We climbed over the ridge tops, along the ledge
clinging to the cliff face until we found a cave.
The sky was luminous. There were small left-over
wisps of cloud, blood streaked by the set sun; then
the darkening light folding us in blacknesses.

It was a goat-herd woke us. We were slumbering
out of our skins, in the pre-alluvial dawn
when we heard them skittering on loose shale
munching the scruff around the cave mouth.

Afterwards, before the sun came up, we saw
in the shadows of the rock-face, the face of Moses.
Over there, the forehead with the brow furrowed
and below, the eyes still closed. The cheeks a pale
red ochre, turning yellow with morning; and the beard
falling away where the waterfall fanned out.

Elijah was next to him. That's what Peter said:
'just as we'd seen him in our ancestors eyes.'
All I saw was greenery, a few bushy outcrops,
they could have been mistaken for eyebrows.
At that moment James came round a corner.
He'd been picking wild cranberries.

And then, as the sun splintered over the rim
Your face, impossibly bright, transparent with memory.
Not a single thing was hidden, everything translucent
simple, holier than we could imagine.

And in the silence: the tenor voice of small streams,
the far-away bass of the waterfall,
a single bird-note, and among them
the word Beloved.

THE LONG ROAD TO LONDON

It was the rusted tongs by the hearth and the jackdaw's nest in the chimney
and the bellows lying on the floor and the broken hasp on the window
and the ghosts of ghosts in the hall and the onions hung from the rafters
and the pair of pewter plates that blindly gaped from the dresser

It was the draught in the wooden stairs and the silences from the landing
and the cobwebbed beams of the roof and the musty smell from the chamber
and the blue tinge of the cheese and the crumbs on the big oak table
and the turnip rind on the floor and the rats running in from the stables

It was the creak of the rotting door and the sound of a horse and carriage
and the powder's purple smell and the reek of ale from the soldier
and the lantern's leaded lights and the way that his face looked swollen
and the wrought iron gate and the hedge and the long road to London

IRISH MICE WIN DESIGN AWARD

They pitter-pattered it to him on a plate, he said.
It was clear as raindrops, the way it was hinted at:
the configurations beside the skirting board
the pattern of the droppings; their skittering
along the zig zag of the wall-paper, their upside-downs
on the underside of the cross beams, their disappearance
through the cracks in the ceiling boards. And all that
without the aid of a step ladder or a tuning fork.
Not even a watering can. It was all the same to him:
the Celtic crosses, the calligraphy, the bog philosophy.
It came to him of a sudden he said. All he did was copy.

JASPER

Lying there on the green couch
I drift into the equilibrium of sleep.
I'm running through a tunnel of evergreens
towards a temple with a shine on its stone steps
their sharp edges transient as rivers
– it could be Venice – and then climbing
into a bell tower that becomes a hedge
beyond which a train approaches
steady as the beat of an old song
and from a grassy mound, your voice
clear as daybreak, reaches across
the frozen lake to the glacier.
We're the age we always were.
I awake to the residue, the dream
already silk scarf, snow-melt.

SEVEN STAINLESS STEEL CONES

Sculpture Garden Canberra

Coming up close he sees what the cones see
– if their feedback is anything to go by.

On his left, a barrel-chested man with ominously widening shoulders,
his muscle-bunched squashed legs as short as a leprechaun's.

On his right, an elongated human string whose hands reach to his knees
but with slim and graceful legs; the miler he once thought he'd be.

In the background there are trees consistent with each scene:
squat and stunted stumps, or stretched up to the skies.

On the outside, disembodied, the one who sees: the Rodins,
the Henry Moore, the sulphur crested cockatoo.

Staying off screen, inspired or self deluded
he conjures up an endless multiplicity of selves.

BRAINS OF A TEAPOT

Whoever thought that up hasn't met my teapot.
Each morning as we sit here watching each other
the shine on this stainless steel Stellar misses nothing.
It takes in each detail then transforms it into its own shape.
The kitchen is re-arranged in a semi circle, so everything
has its place in reverse order. To my left the cooker,
then the orange tea caddy, microwave, toaster, kettle;
to my right the round mouth of the washing machine
brought close, the back door pushed into the shadows.

The window behind me is miniatured into a curve
through which the green line of damson trees
is illuminated by a small band of brightness.
The blue-patterned ceramic trivet it sits on
is imbedded in an inch-high border round its base.
On the table's rounded redness the sugar bowl
is elongated, the jug transformed into a delicate vase
its neck ringed in a calligraphy of bright colours.
The peacock on the egg-cup is perfectly poised.

And here, hunched over my pad, my pen
elegant and tall, my hands the same size
as my head, even my scribble looks exotic
in my looking back teapot, expanded at the top
and at the bottom narrowing to a tiny footpath.
And when I lift it to pour my tea the kitchen tilts,
becomes a chandelier, then goes through the roof.
Everything returns to normal when I set it down.
All this as well as keeping the tea hot.

IN REVERSE

I don't know how I do it, or when it was
I learned. I've always been able. You see
I read maps backwards. Someone draws me
a map, I have to look at it in a mirror. I see it
left to right. Back to front. Maybe that's why.
I can write backwards as well, just as easily
as the other way round, and it's no less
of a scrawl. I did it for the kids
to show how clever I was.
They'd run off looking for a mirror.
Once, Thomás just turned the page over
and read it from the back. Clever kid that.
But, what I was coming to: I'm known
as an erratic driver, and I can't cut bread
straight, but I can reverse into a space
the size of a stamp. I don't know how.
I just take one look, and no matter
how tight, I'm in there first go. I think
it's to do with the way I angle my neck.
I end up a whisper from the kerb, and
exactly parallel. Six inches to spare
front and back. I do it best
when I'm alone.

ARRIVING BACK

Arriving back in twenty-one-sixteen
I couldn't believe how our house had shrunk
And I'd forgotten entirely about the way
People put flowers in jars to brighten up the kitchen.
I'd forgotten the kitchen as well of course,
That they still used gas, and old forms of electricity:
Sockets on the walls wired up to switchboards
With cables running in from underground.

Getting back in forty-two-seventeen
I couldn't get over how the land was barren,
Vast plains of nothingness, dry rock and dust.
I couldn't think what people did for leisure,
Not a golf course in sight, or a swimming pool.
I couldn't take in how children rummaged
In the dust, and licked the rocks for chemicals.
Imagine washing. Imagine taking bird-baths.

When I got back in sixty-three-eighteen
I had no recollection of what talking was.
We'd long since dispensed with conversation.
We'd got used to giving signals with our eyes.
I couldn't remember the shape of written words
Or what they sounded like. How did people
Get consensus on what words meant?
Anyone can read a look.

When I get back in eighty-four-nineteen
I'll try to separate the invention of the wheel
From the splitting of the atom, Neolithic life from air-flight.
I'll differentiate between the Trojan wars and the Crusades,
Sub-aquatic skirmishes and the latest Laser wipe-outs.
I'll search for coastlines, track down where rivers went.
My worry is: millennia may be vacuum packed
Making everything look equally antique.

BEACHCOMBING

after George Mackay Brown

On day one a pair of dolphins appear. They swim parallel to the shore.
We watch each other then they are gone. I see them no more.

On day two I search the shingles and find a flat blue stone.
I skim it into the shimmer of waves; lose it in the sun.

On day three I sail out of Boston on board the Whaler Catalpa.
Our mission: the rescue of Fenian convicts off Freemantle.

On the fourth day a fine-figured blonde woman walks my way.
I see the skin of her neck is shrivelled, her face half eaten away.

On the fifth day a hermit crab crawls out of his shell.
In time he'll grow another. I'll have the original.

On day six at dawn a black woman walks out of the sea.
Says she is Queen Esther; she'll heal me under the medicine tree.

On day seven I read about scalping in Texas in 1849
A white horse rides by with pink fetlocks, blood-orange mane.

On the eighth day a waiter in Mickey Mouse gear says the food is good.
Five hundred percent better than yesterday. Guaranteed.

Sundown, day nine, the incessant sound of an African drum.
Prevent-us-from-error. Prevent-us-from-error. From-error. Amen.

UNDERPASS

The railings ripple, wagon wheels spinning backwards
in an old movie. On a blue sign, a matchstick man
follows the arrow pointing down.

In the underpass a street cleaner in donkey jacket
sits beside his brush under a graffiti rainbow.
You walk quickly, hearing echoes:

a bridle path beside a canal near Selby:
hoof-marks, a fisherman under a canopy,
reeds on the far bank, the water still as Sunday;

Lake Michigan: the icicles pointing upwards,
'Life's a bitch and then you die', the graffiti says,
'my parents screwed me up good,' the girl says.

Long after the waves have forgotten their frozen bulk
you meet her again. She tells you she had planned
to take her life; the lake was frozen too far out.

A doctor by now, walking along some pathway
with her children. A sign: 'no dogs' reminds her
of the lakeside. You emerge out of the underpass.

THE ACCIDENT

i.m. John A. Walsh

Autumn came early that year.
Walking in Wales – the Black Mountains –
Caught in the first snowfall. Thick flurries
Followed by bright sun. I took my shirt off.
There I am with the snowball, showing off my tan.

We stopped at Merthyr Tydfil, had steaks at the Berni Inn
Then headed back North about ten.
You always turned sentimental on those long night journeys,
College days and all that, then you'd start the Rosary.
I dropped you off near Manchester around three.

Driving over the top on the brand new M62
I take the turn off for Sowerby Bridge.
I can't tell you in what order it all broke out:

Climbing up from the gully out of the wreck
Or rolling over and over before coming to rest.
Seeing the blue lights flashing upside down,
Or the shuddering of wheels on the cattle grid.
The policeman's calm voice: 'Are you alright?
Are you alone? You don't have to say anything
But anything you do say...' and so on.

It's all clear now, thirty two years later:
Picking up the golf clubs strewn along the slip road,
Whispers of cold air on my neck.
Pulling my jacket through the back window
The sound of glass on the road when I give it a shake.

TREAD SOFTLY

Under the gardening trousers and a carrier bag
from The Man's Shop, a pair of metal shoe horns
that came with the 'almost new' dead man's shoes
I bought for a quid in 1978,
from the deaf-and-dumb shoemaker on Idle Road.

Footshape Works. Barratt & Co. Northampton.
Adjustable. Size 5-7. Calligraphy on stainless steel.
Their joints, not arthritic yet, had a leather squeak.
Their heels the shape of the shoemaker's chin,
their insteps were clean shaven and slim.

I wore the shoes for years, until a summer night
outside ASDA getting into my car, one of them
came apart. I see him smile as he read my lips,
then shake his head, carve out with his mouth
the consonants he couldn't cut: 'ka-put.'

DELAYED

Breathless as if running up steps
or in a tizz getting ready for Mass

chalice – paten – hosts – water & wine
trying to keep the altar servers to a whisper

while all the time it was only because
I missed my turn off at Ainley Top

and had to drive all the way up the moors
past the place where the motorway splits

because the man who played the tin whistle
wouldn't let them through his house in 1967

to the exit at Saddleworth and the cattle grid
where I got turned over in 1971

then all the way back along the reservoir
seventeen miles to the very same spot

and trying to make up for lost time
I took what I thought was a short cut

past the Infirmary the Children's Library
the man walking his dog, the street littered

with the smell of last night's fish and chips
to these traffic lights stuck forever on red.

COLD HILL POND

There are things it's not necessary to know.
The depth of the pond for instance. Who cares?
Its depth is upwards. The mirror it makes
Is what matters, and what that mirrors:

The movement of clouds. The wide canopy of trees
Before the leaves fall. The double breasted swan
Still as sadness, her domed wings rippled
Contemplative, the tips joined in prayer.

This pond is not for swimming. It's for seeing
What is in the sky and what is not in the sky:

The bales of straw, stacked and square
Like turrets of a Taj Mahal,
The peleton of Canada geese flying south,
Away from the blank cold, away from
The minus of things, to wherever
The swan imagines. I'm glad

It sits beside this twist of road
Each time I take the corner, too fast
For the fact of silence, for the depth of its
Imagining, for the slow heartbeat of the sun.

RETURNING

On the way back I was ablaze.
I was the white light that hits
coming up out of the pothole.
I was a dazzle to myself.

I was at last the fossil-filled
Framework of myself.
Because I said what I said,
because I blurted it out.

And for the first time on this earth
I was standing in my own shoes,
on the other ground of myself.
I was mine. Entirely mine.

Pulling into the service area
I looked out over the lake
and let myself spread
as far as I could.

I rang you and said I was
sorry, then sat at the lakeside
breathing in everything
for which I was not sorry.

ON NOT BEING A SINGER

I've always wanted to be a singer,
To let my voice follow the song as far as it could,
Glide out over the crowd. I can do it alright in my head.
Last night in the mirror inside the sacristy door I was
Ray Charles. *I can't stop loving you.* It was perfect.
Except for the voice, and the fact that I wasn't black.

Willie Nelson. Maybe I could do that, or Pavarotti,
The way he belted it out before the world cup.
But not like the old tramp on O' Connell Street that night
Before the All Ireland: his arms outstretched, head thrown back,
His slurred eyes oblivious to the crowds as they streamed past,
And no sound whatsoever coming out of his mouth.

My father was a fine singer. His father before him
Taught all his children to sing. As a boy he had wanted to
Go off and sing like Caruso, as John Mc Cormack did later on.
He stayed on the farm, and raised thoroughbred horses instead.
My uncles and aunts could all sing. My father's songs were
Hard times come again no more, and *The ship that never returned*.

IS IT YOURSELF?

After the race I go to the unsaddling enclosure.
The horse ran well. The owner's had an each-way bet.
He's satisfied enough. After the jockeys have weighed in
I'm invited to the owner/trainer bar. I listen as they
talk the talk. He'll come on for this. Good to soft
is what he likes. The ground last time out was heavy.
Beyond us, in the large wall mirror: the trainer,
the owner and the owner's friend, and beyond them
out of the corner of my eye an older man, smart jacket,
white hair, handsome, standing just behind me.
Discreetly I turn my head. There's no one there.
In the mirror I look again, this time full on.
He's there alright. Dark Jacket. White hair.

SCARF

I left it in the Malt Shovel in Lambourne.
You'd bought it for me at Machu Picchu
that time I was having the new heart valve.
I loved the blue of it, and the silver threads
running through it like traffic lines at night.
What I'm remembering now is its softness
and the way I left it after me in the pub.

Some punter picked it up. I watched him
wrapped in it at Kempton on Boxing Day,
Clare Balding interviewing him on T.V.
before the King George. 'Nice scarf'
she says. 'Llama wool,' he tells her.
'Someone left it in the Malt Shovel.
Here's hoping it brings me luck.'

ECLIPSE

i.m. Mary Jerry Connie

Laid out there in your narrow box
your face gone small
the spitten image of your mother.

She, your father, all before you
were a fright for the pishogues
the faeries and the long dead:

– A woman washing her hands
in a bucket outside the back door.
– Voices above in the stall

doing nobody any harm.
– Lights below in the bog on a dark night
signalling from the other side!

I was never too sure about any of that
at least not since I was small.
What I am certain of

I was standing at our front door
waiting for the eclipse of the sun
when I heard the news that you were gone.

Looking up the field just after 11.00am
the birds going silent, the light getting dim,
a black heifer of Jerry Neill's turned into a man.

The neck and head grew out of
its hind quarters, it had one pair of legs!
What would the ould crowd have thought of that?

What I thought of was
the day fifty years ago,
when you came to prepare the house for a wake.

Washing the statue of the Sacred Heart,
and four year old me saying
'don't tickle him neck'

puzzled that my brother James
was lying like a statue
above in the bed.

Now you're gone wherever we go
when we leave what we have here.
The birds have stopped singing for good.

May you be among your own.
Rewarded for a kindness done.
Rarer than an eclipse of the sun.

THE TOWN

Brazen, they said, brazen,
the way the pair of them paraded
up and down the town, without an ounce
of shame on them, their skirts barely covering
their knees; head-lamps you never saw the like of.
'Them two will have no bother getting husbands,
if they last that long.' They both married young.

Today I saw one of them, I'm almost certain
meandering down Main Street. Moving slowly,
ponderous. A grandmother by now.

While up in North Street, Minihane's Public House
is as it always was. The narrow doorway, and inside
my father drinking porter with old men, as they talk
about the troubles. Kilmichael, Crossbarry,
how they beat the Black and Tans.

The back yard down to the river is overgrown,
the stables derelict. But the tide is in, and if
I close my eyes, I'll smell the horse manure,
hear the far off tinkle of harness bells.

PORTRAIT

after Cagley Robinson

The lakeshore curves to the shape
of an angel's waist. A medallion moon
sends its blood-orange beam across the water
to where the sheep gather and the shepherds
with their lamp and water-jar watch over them.
The girl shepherd is barefoot, holding a lamb,
her free hand circles the white bark of a beech.
Behind, a cluster of boulders offer them shelter.

*

Christmas is coming and knife crime is down
the statistics claim. Which is what Herod said
to the three wise men before he sent his soldiers
with knives to carry out what they were good at.
Blood splatters the uneven streets of Ramah again,
Rachel weeping for her children. The commander
calls it hysteria, as the Red Cross are kept at bay
and absent cameras silence the decibels of grief.

*

Meanwhile, you write your long haul Christmas cards,
remembering Lake Michigan: how the waters froze
until stalagmites lined along the Chicago shoreline,
recalling the stalactite candelabras of your childhood
the wax-melt drooping over turnip candle-stands
in the lit windows of farmhouses across the valley.
Toureen, Lissane and Bawnahow. Willie Paul's.
Jerry Charley's. Dan Dan's. Michael Paddy's.

THE APPOINTMENT

Inside, the sun throws colours down the aisle.
Outside, pigeons shuffle on a window ledge.
Inside, the high altar, the carved statues of kings.
Outside, the river, the city walls, the bridge.

Inside, the rose window, intimations of heaven.
Outside, the Shambles where Margaret Clitheroe lived.
Inside, the west door carvings you caress with your fist.
Outside, the stone archway leading to the Purey Cust.

In here, the table mirror you look down into
To see the roof. In there, the scanner you peer at
To see your heart. The great cross-beams, restored
After the fire. The mitral valve that doesn't work.

Afterwards, the falling leaves, the bench where you sit.
The plaque in memory of Eric and Edna Smith.

PASSING OUT

As I relate how
the sudden loss of balance
unbalanced me, how the nausea spread
until my face could feel itself turning
from colourless to turquoise white

how I hovered this side of passing out
having no say in anything until
the doctor came, and how
lying in the ambulance
it seemed to head in the wrong direction

I remember that after I'd let go of worrying
it occurred to me: if this is how we take our leave
it is less distressing than some things
I can think of, say unrequited love
or missing a train.

PATIENT

Knowing how I hate hospitals, I try to
distract myself with people whose plight
is worse than mine. William Trevor's
Beyond the pale and other stories.

It doesn't work. Noticing the elderly couple
opposite, I next peruse the colour scheme
the lighting, the glass-topped double doors.
Through them, down a long corridor I see
security guards with guard dog approaching.
I can't actually see the dog, just the dog chain.
A security man is holding it with both hands.

Coming through the doors into full view,
they're not security guards, and it's not a dog,
and the man in the green surgical gown
is not a medic. He is handcuffed to the chain
which is handcuffed to a guard. They lead him
up the stairs and out of sight. Voyeurs
caught in the act we look away.

Someone out of prison tells me later
his dread of hospital appointments.
The most humiliating part: how people
out of pity, turned their heads away.

MISTAKEN IDENTITY

Venturing out that first time after surgery
walking slowly, protective of my middle
I pass the red brick terraces on Carville Road
and on down to the High Street, where I see
in Greenwoods plate-glass window
among sweaters and manikins in pink shirts
my uncle who died in 1975, looking out at me
with searching eyes, wearing my clothes.

CUTTING ASPARAGUS TIPS

They seem to have grown overnight,
in the silence between
bird song and birdsong,
among the still reaches of the moon.

Cut them now, before they grow wild!
Back inside I scan the drawer
for the knife with the serrated edge
until I spot its black handle.

I slice each stick sideways. The blade
passes sweetly through the soft flesh
of the fat ones. Through the spindly ones
it grates, like a bicycle over stones.

So much growth again: the Virginia creepers
closing in on the windows, crowding
round the door-frame; the thorn hedge
thickening. I liked all that last year,

even the grass sprouting between the flagstones.
This time I resist its urgency
object to its violent insistence.
There is no stopping it.

I never saw what the cancer looked like,
but a woman who watched the cloud
mushrooming over Hiroshima said:
'it was very beautiful'.

Discovered in the same week
my first poem was published.
Did it look like asparagus tips?
Was its appearance beautiful?

I was somewhere else when they
cut it out. But that horizontal stripe
below my navel is still decorated
by the surgeon's serrated stitch-marks.

A DREAM OF WHITE FLOWERS

Someone is putting flowers round the bed
Where I'm sleeping. Someone is saying
How much I'm welcome.

Awakening, though not yet awake
Hospitality seeps into me. Penetrates
My shield of disbelief. Of late

I've been alien to myself.
So-what-ing my accomplishments.
I have lived in that cold climate.

And now visited by friends
And now this dream! I am
Knit back into my history.

The bed is large, luxuriant.
The duvet cover warm and dark.
The flowers – there are lots of them – all white.

VOLIVOLI

The spit of white sand washed smooth,
tiny holes where the crabs have hidden,
the sea glistening green over the coral reef.

Night now and a breeze brushes my face,
a mongoose skitters across the grass,
hibiscus sway, an overhanging branch

splintering the moonlight. A head-high shape
accompanied by its shadow, but no footsteps:
a towel hanging on a clothes-line.

There are no sounds, as if the sea itself sleeps.
Below, the fish who never sleep: Barracuda,
Sweet lips, Coral Trout. Mantas in the deep.

Above, the half moon over the mangroves.
Its slanted light has turned the sea to milk.

DUET

In the dream you come towards me
dark hair curled about your neck
your smile a bright innocence.

I take in my two hands
the melodeon of your rib-cage
and the music between us begins.

Awake now, my whole being
is glad. Longing still lingers
on my fingertips.

AT THE RACES

7 July 2007

In the dream my nephew, who is called after me
meets me at the races. He tells me I'm on yesterday's video.
I remember yesterday, and where I was among the crowd.
I was in the grass paddock beside the hayshed,
standing on a rock above the furze machine.
It was around 1957. 'There you are' he says,
pointing up at the big screen.

I see myself coming towards me.
I'm wearing that checked grey overcoat.
I walk out of the screen past myself and notice
the overcoat is baggy. I'm bulkier than I thought.
As I walk up the terrace steps I observe myself
from the back. My hair is standing up. Thicker
than I remember. It's turning from grey to black.

When I look again at the screen the video is finished.
I want to see the playback. The remote is out of reach.
I'm looking for a window-opener, or that long handled
candle-snuffer, when a woman asks me if she can help.
She gets the tape, a reel to reel, puts it into the machine.
I ask if it can be fast forwarded. She says not.
I'll have to watch it from the start.